D0458284

Acclaim for Stu Weber's original, full-length book, *Tender Warrior*

"Stu Weber challenges us to be the men that God intended. For the sake of our wives, our children, and our nation, I hope that every American male will read and heed this memorable book."

DAN COATS
FORMER U.S. SENATOR, INDIANA

"*Tender Warrior* provides hope for men by challenging their assumptions and shaping their convictions. Read it. Devour it. Then live it. This is the time for real men to emerge."

DENNIS RAINEY
EXECUTIVE DIRECTOR, FAMILYLIFE AND COAUTHOR OF *GROWING A SPIRITUALLY STRONG FAMILY*

"I drank Budweiser, smoked Marlboros, and chased women.... *Tender Warrior* sent me deeper into my heart and soul. When I finished it I passed it on to a (sorry) friend, who was supposed to give it back, but passed it on to someone else (even sorrier). This book changed his life. It knocked down the walls around his heart. His response: 'The most important thing that has happened in my life started when you sent me that book.'"

A READER

The Heart

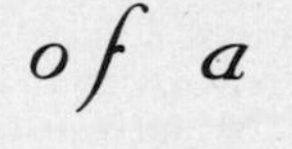

of a

Tender Warrior

LifeChange Books

Stu Weber

Multnomah Books

THE HEART OF A TENDER WARRIOR
published by Multnomah Books
A division of Random House, Inc.

International Standard Book Number: 978-1-59052-039-0

Cover design by The Office of Bill Chiaravalle
Cover image by Stockart.com

Printed in the United States of America

For information:
MULTNOMAH BOOKS
12265 ORACLE BOULEVARD, SUITE 200
COLORADO SPRINGS, CO 80921

Library of Congress Cataloging-in-Publication Data
Weber, Stu.
The heart of a tender warrior / Stu Weber.
p. cm.
Includes bibliographical references.
ISBN 1-59052-039-4
1. Christian men--Religious life. 2. Masculinity--Religious aspects--Christianity. I. Title.
BV4528.2 .W425 2002
248.8'42--dc21 2002005550

08—10 9 8 7 6 5 4 3

Dedication

To Kevin Jones,
always a warrior,
a competitive son of thunder,
who discovered a tender heart and
showed us all how to face the last great
enemy of the soul with courage, tenacity, and
an uplifting smile.

"Death is swallowed up in victory.
O Death, where is your victory?
O Death, where is your sting?"

CONTENTS

One

WAKE-UP CALL

HOW MANY TIMES can a man hear a wake-up call without waking up? Some men, I suppose, never do. This man almost didn't.

I've had two major wake-up calls at two crossroads in my life. Neither was much like the gentle ring of an alarm clock. Both were more akin to the crack of a two-by-four across the back of my skull.

The first call came in the heat and terror of Vietnam. I was the Group Intelligence Officer, serving the Fifth Special Forces Group. My responsibilities included briefing "the old man," Colonel "Iron Mike"

Healy, on the enemy situation around our A-Team camps from the Delta in the south to the DMZ in the north. Very few young captains had access to the entire country as I did. Very few could grab aircraft when needed. It was heady stuff for a twenty-five-year-old from Yakima, Washington.

My wake-up call came one spring, on a hillside. We were at Dak Pek, at the northern end of the Dak Poko Valley in the central highlands. My face was pushed into the muddy banks of a small trench at the perimeter of a Special Forces A-Camp.

Something was out there. Something big. And we knew it. All the indicators were there. We'd been picking them up for days—consistent "hostile" contact with our patrols, increased radio traffic (only "big boys" had such radios in the North Vietnamese Army), and a real upsurge in other tactical intelligence in the area. Even the informant "agent nets" began to pick up abnormal numbers of clues.

They were out there all right. And we were their target. Overrunning a Special Forces A-Camp was a prime trophy for any NVA big shot.

In some ways the waiting was almost as bad as being under attack. Just knowing that several companies of crack North Vietnamese regulars were out there on the perimeter—waiting for the right moment to come screaming out of the forest—turned life into a waking nightmare. There in that muddy ditch—reeling from the fears and threats of imminent combat—it finally caught up to me. I finally heard the wake-up call. In that moment, I faced up to the very real possibility that I would never go home. That I might not beat the odds. My life might indeed end in that faraway place. It might not be "someone else" leaving that valley in a body bag, flying home in a silver flag-draped coffin.

I could actually die. Within hours. Possibly even minutes. As I grappled with those thoughts, a question burned its way to the surface of my mind. After smoldering in my soul for months, the question now burst into hot flame.

What matters? What really matters?

If a young captain by the name of Stuart K. Weber died in the Dak Poko Valley, what would he have accomplished during his quarter century on earth? What was life all about, anyway?

Called back to Nha Trang, I caught a helicopter out of Dak Pek, missing the worst of the battle. Our little camp was virtually blasted from the face of the planet. Eventually the siege lifted, and the NVA crawled away to lick their wounds. Our guys loaded up the wounded, collected the dead, and began to build the camp all over again. Somehow, for some reason, I'd been handed yet one more chance to wake up and open my eyes.

And this time I did. I began rethinking my life. Again I went back to duty. But I was never the same. The spiritual roots of my childhood, long abandoned during the social and intellectual turmoil of the sixties, began to take hold in my heart. The faith of my father and grandfather sent pilings deep into my soul. I realized that Jesus Christ was exactly who He said He was. He became very real to me, and life changed from that day.

A SECOND WAKE-UP CALL

If you're a married man, you'll understand my second life-changing wake-up call. If you're still single, take my word for it: This was a moment every bit as intense as that first wake-up call in the muddy trench at Dak Pek. This one didn't come out of the sky like a mortar shell, but it did come "out of the blue." Actually, it flashed out of Linda's eyes. For the first time in our fifteen years of marriage, I saw anger there. Deep, hot anger. It wasn't like Linda, and that made it unmistakable.

It was absolutely clear—there would be changes in our relationship, or our relationship would change. Things were never going to be the same.

I began to realize some things. It seems I had been taking our relationship for granted. Looking back, I realized I'd been treating her more like a trophy (conquered and on the shelf) than a companion. More like a contractual partner than a friend with whom to share my insides. The signals had been there, but...I hadn't seen them. Typical guy.

How had we come to such a morass? Why did marriage in those early days shape up more like combat than companionship? Over time I came to find out it had to do with *manliness*—or the lack of it. Finally understanding how the living God put me together as a man has helped us grow as a couple.

And—whether you are married or not—manliness is what this little book is all about. Real, God-made, down-in-the-bedrock masculinity is something men in our culture struggle to understand. Tough? Tender? Strong? Sensitive? Fierce? Friendly? Which is it? We're frustrated. Often confused. Sometimes irritable. But determined. Determined to discover our manhood and live it to the hilt.

Maybe you've already experienced a couple of wake-up calls in the course of your life. Listening to the whistle of incoming mortar shells or looking into the furious eyes of the only woman you've ever loved can certainly open a fellow's eyes.

Chances are, you won't need the kind of alarm bells it took to pry me out of slumber. As a matter of fact, our gracious God might even choose to use a little book like this to accomplish something very big in your life, without all that trauma.

So let's just consider this your first wake-up call....

Take It to Heart:

Along the way, every one of us will find ourselves in situations that shake us to the core—and cause us to think about the critical issues of life. But why wait until circumstances crush us? *Now* is the time to wake up and seek God's help, wisdom, and direction.

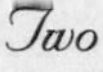

The Scout

IF YOU WERE GLUED to the tube as I was in the late fifties and early sixties, you may remember a Western called *Wagon Train.* It always opened with the stocky, fatherly Ward Bond astride his mustang, squinting with wind-chiseled features into the horizon. With a quick look back over his shoulder, he would raise a rawhide-gloved right hand in a beckoning gesture and call out, "Wagons, *ho-oh!*"

Bond was perfect as Seth Adams, the gruff but kind-hearted wagon master. I loved the way he commanded that great prairie train snaking its way across the wide plains.

But the guy I really wanted to see came galloping up next. Clad in fringed buckskins and a wide-brimmed black hat, he rode up alongside the wagon master at the head of the train. As the theme music rolled on, the black-and-white television screen filled with the image of the lithe-limbed, cleft-chinned, raven-haired Robert Horton as Flint McCullough.

The Scout. Oh man, those were the cowboy boots I wanted to step into. That was the job I wanted. It was Flint McCullough who always rode miles out in front of that long, ponderous caravan. Flint McCullough, the ever vigilant eyes and ears of the wagon train...probing out ahead, checking out the trail, looking for Indians, scouting out water holes, scanning the shimmering skyline with young eyes made old and wise by the miles he had ridden and the things he had seen. He was the first to smell danger, dodge the arrows, hear the muted thunder of faraway buffalo herds, and taste the bite of distant blizzards riding the prairie wind. It was up to him to spot potential hazards, discern lurking enemies, and pick out the best and safest trail for the train to follow.

The immigrants in their wagons couldn't see all the dangers ahead. They couldn't imagine what threatened over the next rise. They didn't know where to find water for their barrels or grass for their livestock. They had to rely on The Scout.

It's always the image of Flint McCullough that swims into my mind as I think about the role of a man in today's world. It all centers on the word *provision.* Now that wouldn't make much sense if you thought only of the traditional definition of *provider.* In our culture, when we think of *provision,* we think of food on the table and a roof over our heads. Actually, the emphasis in *provision* is *vision.* The *pro* part of the word indicates "before" or "ahead of time." *Vision* obviously speaks of "sight" or "seeing."

What does that formula yield? Looking ahead. Giving direction. Anticipating needs. Defining the destination. Riding ahead of the wagon on scout duty.

What makes a man? Above all else, it is *vision.* A vision for something larger than himself. A vision of something out there ahead. A vision of a place to go, a cause to serve. Call it a hill to climb, a mountain to conquer, a continent to cross, a dream glimmering way out there on the horizon. Call it what you will, but at its heart, it's vision. A man must visualize ahead of time. Project. Think forward. Lift his eyes and chart the course ahead. Ask leading questions. Picture the future. Anticipate what the months and years may bring. This is the very essence of his leadership. This is the "king" in every man...always looking ahead, watching out for his people, providing direction and order.

Physical provision for the needs of a family are actually the easiest duties of the provisionary. A little food, a little shelter, and physical provision is a done deal. But that isn't *real* provision. Thinking that food, clothing, and shelter equal provision is like confusing sex with love. Yes, it's a rather significant part of the story, but it isn't the whole book.

As men, we so often misplace our vision. We focus myopically on houses and cars and stock portfolios and bank accounts and piling up "stuff." We imagine that we find status and security in such things, when, in reality, there is no status or security if we don't have relationships. We tell ourselves, "If I have a financial plan, if I've tucked away some money for college, if I have a good life-insurance policy, I'm being a good provider." We revert to the things we can see, when, in fact, it is the *unseen* world, the world of the spirit, the world of relationships, where we ought to be majoring in our provision. The matters of character—heart, spirit, integrity, justice, humility—will last when everything else has turned to dust. These are the character traits that outlive a man and leave not a monument, but a legacy.

What confidence that kind of masculine leadership brings—to a military unit, to an organization, to a family, to a church!

MAN ON THE SCENE

One of the strongest impressions I had growing up in central Washington was experiencing the presence of a man who always seemed to know where he was going. Because Pastor O. H. Williams knew why he was there and what he was about, I felt an enveloping sense of security every time I stepped through the doors of our little church. If he was there, everything was going to be okay. Kingdoms could rise and fall...no problem. Even if a meteor crashed through the roof of the church on Sunday morning, and there was total chaos, he would know just what to do. He always seemed to be able to look down the road to see what was coming. And when the time came to take action on something, you always knew Pastor Williams would be in the lead, instructing and encouraging in that warm, steady, competent voice of his.

Whenever he was on vacation, a vague uneasiness rippled through the ranks. People felt skittish. Restive. Out of sync. But when O. H. was back on the platform, a palpable sense of relief washed through the building. We could face whatever with calm certainty. The man was back.

Too many married guys squander that respect and leadership—and then wonder why they lose their families.

It's the all too common downside to superficial definitions of "success." Don't let anyone snow you—*nothing* makes up for the failure of a family. At the heart of a real man's purpose is the health of his family. If you have a family *that's your job.* You're The Scout. You set the vision.

A man's wife has wonderful vision, too, and can scan the skyline with the best of them, if she needs to. But the Creator in His wisdom has uniquely equipped her to see things *close-up,* the details of making that wagon a secure and comfortable refuge.

A man's children may be bright and intelligent, but hey, they're in new territory. They're on strange turf. They have no idea what they'll be facing over the next rise. They romp and play and cut-up alongside the wagon as it pitches along, without a thought for deadly hazards and cruel enemies.

They're all looking to you, The Scout. They're depending on you to set the course, to determine the direction, to set the pace. They're looking to you for advance warning of storms, flash floods, box canyons, bottomless swamps, and waterless valleys ahead.

The measure of a married man is the spiritual and emotional health of his family. A real provider has a vision for a marriage that bonds deeply, for sons with character as strong as trees, and for daughters with confidence and deep inner beauty. Without that vision and leadership, a family struggles, gropes, and may lose its way.

What do you do when you're lost in the woods? You climb a tree! There *is* fresh air up there, you know. There is direction and wisdom and landmarks that will never change. A man *can* get the perspective he needs to step into a leadership role...if he is willing to humble himself and seek it from the Lord God. Consider the counsel of James: "But if any of you lacks wisdom, let him ask of God, who gives to all men generously and without reproach, and it will be given to him" (James 1:5).

Men, if you find yourself or your family lost in the woods, maybe it's time for you to climb a tree. Maybe it's time for you to get your head above the limbs and leaves, take a deep breath of fresh air, and scan the purple hills in the distance. The provisionary must know the difference between the forest and the trees. He needs to scale the heights from time to time, and, with God's help, see the horizon.

It's not that men are genetically farsighted while women are nearsighted. It has more to do with the God-given tendency of a man to look up and out and discern objects in the hazy distance and the tendency of a woman to read the fine print of relationships. A woman is simply a better reader. She has a better focus on people and situations near at hand. She can read right away what's happening in the spirit, in a tone of voice, in a fleeting facial expression. That's why she so often tugs at a man. He gets so far out there in his "provision" role that he fails to see things under his very nose! Women place more emphasis on details and on security.

Provisionaries need to use their God-given capacity for distance vision to encourage and give hope and security to their families. When they cannot or will not, the people under their roofs suffer loss.

How is it in your household? Does your family share a vision of a mountain-sized goal in the distance, flashing and glistening above the fog of disappointments and daily pressures? Is your wagon rolling toward a lush green valley on the other side of tomorrow? Is your vision wide enough and high enough to keep the old wheels rolling through the dusty, sometimes monotonous plains of this adventure called life?

When you think about it, you don't have much time to step up to your high calling as wagon master and scout. The trek that seems so long now will soon be a memory. But there's time enough. Time enough to take that first step. Time enough to push your way through peripheral issues and life-draining preoccupations and ride out ahead of the family God has given you. Ready to saddle up? Then tighten the cinch, and let's move out.

Wagons, *ho-oh!*

Take It to Heart:

God expects men to be providers in the most complete sense of the word…leaders with eyes on the horizon, anticipating the perils, smelling hope in the wind, and inspiring loved ones to follow.

Three

STAYING POWER

I RECALL MY FIRST extended time away from home. It was my freshman year in college. Having never before been east of Idaho, I now faced the prospect of an entire semester in a strange land called Illinois. It might as well have been Siberia. Or Mars.

For a youngster accustomed to the mountains of the West, it seemed as though Illinois had no horizon. The gray, flat land and the dreary days seemed to drone on into eternity. I wanted nothing more than to come home. I dreamed of it. Longed for it. Framed a thousand valid reasons for bagging school and heading west. But for reasons I couldn't even articulate at the time, I stayed with it.

At last, after months of numbing endurance, I arrived in home country. As I stepped off the train, Dad emerged from the crowd and shook my hand. I'll never forget what he said: "Son, you have something no one can ever take away from you. It's on the inside. You stuck it out. You've done some growing up."

He was right. People, events, evil schemes, disasters, and catastrophes can take things away from you. Things on the outside. But no one can ever take away what's on the inside—heart, soul, character. A man might throw it away, but no one can ever take it away.

What I'm talking about is something longer and stronger than patience. Shining through the darkness of trials and hardships and every difficult circumstance imaginable is what I believe to be a man's greatest strength. His highest attribute. I call it *staying power.*

WHAT IS STAYING POWER?

In a letter to scattered and suffering Christians, James tagged that same quality *endurance.*

> Consider it all joy, my brethren, when you encounter various trials, knowing that the testing of your faith produces endurance. And let endurance have its perfect result, that you may be perfect and complete, lacking in nothing. (James 1:2–4)

A literal rendering yields the phrase *staying under.* Remaining. Persevering. Holding fast. Standing firm. That's what a man does. That's what a man is.

The military equivalent of *staying under* probably finds its ultimate fulfillment in an institution called army Ranger school. As a young military officer, I had been called on to endure unbelievably rigorous training before being shipped out to Southeast Asia. In the middle of my tour in Vietnam, I often wondered: *How on earth could a guy survive this if he didn't have Ranger school?* The whole point of that training was to help us overcome our most basic fears so that we could function no matter what kind of pressure or circumstances we might face in our future duties. The physical, mental, and emotional stress they put us under defies description.

As I pen these words, I can picture our little company at four-thirty in the morning—what we called in the military "oh-dark-thirty"—crawling along on our bellies under logs and through mucky, water-filled trenches. Later afternoon would find us staggering with exhaustion and bleeding from the feet after forced marches of endless miles. And just when we thought we were going to expire, some officer would be in our face screaming, "Drive on, Ranger, *drive on!*"

Through it all we began to find out something about the limits of a man's mind and body. We *could* get along without food, function without sleep, and keep going like that day after day—even on past the end of our frayed rope. They proved to us that we could do what we had to do.

The patriarch Job would have done well in Ranger school. What staying power this man had! Think of it. He was a man whose masculinity rested not in what he owned, not in the size of his home, not in the amount of his investments, not in what he could achieve, not in the people he knew, not in what model donkey he rode, not in his status in the community.

Job proved himself quite apart from decorations and tributes and trophies and newspaper clippings. When everything he had ever valued had been stripped away from him—children, grandchildren, flocks, herds, wealth, servants, reputation, and health—he lifted his tear-stained face to the stars and declared:

"Naked I came from my mother's womb,
and naked I will depart.

The LORD gave and the LORD has taken away;
may the name of the LORD be praised."
(Job 1:21, NIV)

Job sourced his masculinity and personhood in who he was, alone and naked before God. And that makes a man out of you.

There was a sense of permanence in Job. He was strong, stable, secure—consistent throughout. What you saw was what you got—whether he had the visible trappings of God's blessing or not. In sickness and in health, for better or for worse, for richer or for poorer, *Job stayed.* Sounds like a marriage vow, doesn't it? For good reason. You see, that marriage covenant and the spirit of those words are at the core of a man's manhood. A man's greatest strength is his capacity to stay by the stuff. To make and keep promises. A man's word connects...and stays.

At one point, the old patriarch vows, "Though He slay me, yet will I trust Him" (Job 13:15, NKJV). Standing in the fierce winds of hell itself, Job refuses to turn from his commitment. And that is masculinity, pure and unadulterated.

BUT MEN AREN'T STAYING

It is this staying power that makes and marks a man. Not climbing ladders. Not grabbing for gusto. Not frenzied movement. Not making an impression. Certainly not leaving our wives or abandoning our families or disappearing into a fog of passivity. Today's real men are a vanishing breed, and it's killing our culture.

Today, fully one-third of American children live apart from their natural fathers. Over fifteen million kids are growing up in homes without any father. Seventy percent of men in prison grew up without a father.

Often when I read statistics like these, the names of men I have personally known come to mind. Some of those names and faces had been part of the church I pastor. But they are gone now. Gone from their wives, their children, their homes, and their church. I confess that their names bring a measure of disrespect to my mind. I know they experienced pain. I know there was pressure. I know it wasn't easy. I know "there are two sides." But the bottom line is, they cut and ran. They didn't stay. They didn't keep their word. "Till death do us part" was evidently a Hollywood line to them. They wanted to be strong and virile men. But when they ran, what strength they lost!

They were looking for virility, and in thinking they would find it somewhere else, they lost it. But it's still out in front of them like some cruel mirage they'll never reach. For them it wasn't "women and children first," it was *me* first. That's a little boy, not a man. In their frantic chase after "happiness," they lost their manhood, perhaps never to regain it.

THE POWER OF A PROMISE

The ability to make and keep promises is central to manhood. It may be trite to say that a man's word is his bond, but it is never trite to see it in action. It is a man at his best—giving his word and making good on it, making a promise and keeping it. The calling of every man is to offer stability to a world full of chaos. Consistency to a world in flux. Security to an insecure place.

We live in a "hope so" world. There are few certainties in this life. Ours is a world of dreams, hopes, and wishful thinking. We "hope" our ship will come in. We "hope" that our marriages will work out...that we will find fulfillment...that our children will turn out okay...that we'll be able to keep a decent job.

We would love to change our hope to certainty. And we can—in the things that matter. The things inside. A real man brings certainty to his world by the power of a promise.

Promise making and promise keeping are at the

heart of godliness. At the heart of God—at the very core of His nature—is the making and keeping of promises. All of Scripture hangs on a promise, a series of covenants. A man's promise is an awesome power. Lewis Smedes said it well: "When a man makes a promise, he creates an island of certainty in a heaving ocean of uncertainty.... When you make a promise you have created a small sanctuary of trust within the jungle of unpredictablity."[1]

When Grampa Weber used to tell me, "You're a Weber boy," I knew exactly what he meant. It meant you told the truth, and you kept your word. Even though I was just a little chip when he said those words to me, they've echoed in my heart for my entire life. I wanted to live up to being a Weber boy...which meant, *always, always keep your word. When you lose that, you've lost yourself.*

Linda and I were married over thirty-five years ago, and we had not a hint of an inkling of what those years would bring. How could we possibly have imagined what the winds of the years would blow into our lives? War in Vietnam and agonizing separation. Financial pressure. Miscarriage. The stress of ministry. The pain of criticism. The weight of responsibility. And more. When we stood together at the altar that sunny afternoon, we couldn't have guessed a tenth of it.

But we didn't need to. We made a promise. We recited a vow. Out of the whole world, we chose each other. And the power of that choice, that promise, has kept us. There is no question in either of our minds that we could find a "better mate." Does that surprise you? It shouldn't. There is always someone out there better than you. There will always be someone more beautiful, intelligent, wealthy, witty, competent, sensitive, or sensual. But that's a nonissue to Linda and me. The toxin of comparison has been utterly neutralized and washed away by the sacred antitoxin of a promise.

That's staying power.

The bottom line? Stay with it, man. Stick by your commitments. Stand by your promises. Never let go, no matter what. When work is crushing your spirit...*don't let it beat you.* When the local church is overwhelmed with pettiness...*stay by it.* When marriage isn't fun...*stay in it.* When parenting is over your head...*stay at it.* When your children let you down...*pick them up.* When your wife goes through a six-month mood swing...*live with it.* When it's fourth and fourteen with no time on the clock...*throw another pass.*

Understand that the heart of staying power is *sacrifice*—giving oneself up for the good of another. For the ultimate example of staying power, our eyes have only to lock in on the Lord Jesus Christ. When He could have turned away from the cross, He stayed on course, setting His face like flint, all the way to Calvary. When He could have come down from the cross and sidestepped the suffering, He stayed. When He could have summoned armies of angels to deliver Him and called down divine air strikes on His adversaries, He stayed. He persevered and "stayed under" all the way until that moment came when He could cry out, "It is finished!"

And why did He do that? So that through His resurrection power alive in our lives, you and I could become the kind of men He called us to be. We can hang in there and face anything life or death or hell has to throw at us...because He did it all before us. He not only models staying power, He provides it for the asking. He not only shows us what the ultimate man is like, He rolls up His sleeves and helps us get it done.

That's why real men don't run. Real men stay and stay and stay. Like Job. Like Jesus.

Take It to Heart:

The true measure of a man is not in his physical power, in the skill of his hands, in the quickness of his wit, or in his ability to pile up possessions. True, manly courage is best seen in his willingness to make and keep promises—though all hell should oppose him.

Four

BENEATH THE BREASTPLATE

IMAGINE JOHN WAYNE diapering a baby. Or Clint Eastwood "cooing" a toddler. You pretty much *have* to imagine it, because you've probably never seen it on the silver screen. It's not the right image, you know. The celluloid hard guy is hard-core. Scornful of sentiment. One-dimensional. And phony as a guy in a cheap gorilla suit. Hollywood folks wouldn't know a tender warrior if they saw one. They get it wrong every time.

Underneath the warrior's breastplate beats a tender

center. In every man there is a tender side. The side that connects to another. The thirst for relationship. The desire to touch and be touched. To hug. To link. To be *with*.

Contrast Tinsel Town's John Wayne ("Never apologize, mister. It's a sign of weakness.") with real-life hero General Norman Schwarzkopf. Not long after the Gulf War and the dazzling victory over Iraq, the conquering commander of Desert Storm appeared on national television in an interview with Barbara Walters. In the course of their conversation about the war, something touched the big man. We all watched with fascination as the eyes of this career soldier with four stars on his shoulder glazed over. Tears formed.

Ms. Walters, with well-practiced bluntness, said, "Why, General, aren't you afraid to cry?"

Stormin' Norman replied without hesitation, "No, Barbara. I'm afraid of a man who *won't* cry!"

Barbara had more than she bargained for on the other end of her jaded microphone. America was witnessing the distinctive heartbeat of a tender warrior. I'd cheerfully follow him into the back alleys of Baghdad or the caves of Afghanistan. Wouldn't you?

Real men long for connection, touch, and the genuine expression of feelings.

You see it every Sunday during the football season. It's there—among some of the world's biggest, strongest, most competitive men. The inner drive to touch and connect won't be denied. What's the first thing they do when a great offensive drive explodes in a touchdown?

They look for someone to touch. Oh sure, it might be a cheerful head butt, a smacking of big fists, or a slapping of hands, but they're really disguised hugs. Those magnificent hulks of the gridiron long to be connected. *We did this together. I like you. You like me. We're teammates. We belong. Let's touch...if only for a second and just a little bit.*

It's the tender side trying to shine through the warrior. But it's often just a momentary burst. Our false images of manliness will try to shut it down.

Now don't get me wrong. There is a world of difference between *tender* and *soft.* I'm not at all advocating what Robert Bly calls the "soft male" of the 1970s. We want tender warriors...not "soft males." Webster's Dictionary nicely distinguishes between the terms. *Tender* is linked to the Old French root *tendre,* which means "to stretch out or extend." The word itself is defined as "expressing or expressive of feelings of love, compassion, kindness; affectionate, as in 'a tender caress'; considerate, careful."

In contrast, when the word *soft* is used to describe an individual, it means "mild, effeminate, easily yielding to physical pressure; unresistant to molding, scuffing, wear; untrained for hardship."

Masculine sensitivity never will and never *should* match its feminine counterpart. The average male will never be as sensitive as the average female. Don't even try. Just accept it. Accept your lady's highly developed, finely tuned sensitivities. The difference is part of the Creator's planned complement. So don't overdo. But do loosen up...it's a long way from macho to soft. Come down somewhere in between.

TOUCHED BY A TENDER WARRIOR

I recall one magnificent warrior from my past. He commanded one of the most powerful military units you could hope to see—a five-thousand-man armored brigade. A tank battalion, two mechanized infantry battalions, an artillery battalion, and the Third Squadron of the Twelfth Cavalry. Colonel DeWitt C. Smith knew himself well enough that he was unintimidated by "image"—his own or anyone else's. He was handsome and articulate. A powerful leader and a soldier's soldier.

His Second Brigade of the Third Armored Division sat astride the Fulda Gap at the height of the Cold War.

The Soviet armored units to the east presented a formidable opponent. It was serious stuff.

Colonel Smith applied himself fully to the task. He took his mission seriously, and every man in the brigade knew it. Don't mess with the colonel. Don't mess with the mission. Just don't mess up, period. Get it right.

But the colonel took more than his mission seriously. He took his men seriously. He loved his soldiers. Actually loved them. I was one of them and felt that love. So did my wife. The tender heart of that warrior touched us in a deep and unforgettable way.

Linda was pregnant. Our first. This fuzzy-cheeked second lieutenant and his wife were going to have a baby. We were thrilled. Couldn't wait. I walked taller. Linda smiled more. Life was rich! Plans were in place, and the nursery was taking shape. It was big time.

Then it happened. I was in the field with the brigade on maneuvers. Linda was alone, ten thousand miles from home, mother, and friends. She began to bleed. Then she miscarried—and my young wife's world began to spin like a crazy top, out of control. Another officer's wife with more experience in "military communication" managed to get the message to the maneuvering brigade busy at its serious work.

Colonel Smith called me to his headquarters. My commanding officer met me with a tenderness beyond anything I'd ever observed in him. (Isn't it funny how the less mature feel constrained to act "tough," while the truly mature act gently?)

In a quiet voice, with his eyes locked onto mine, my "CO" began describing what had happened to Linda and our baby. He told me it hurt her. But more than the physical loss, he told me it hurt her inside—at the core of her feminine soul. Most insightfully, he spoke to me of her heart and what he anticipated she was experiencing in her soul. He told this younger soldier, newer husband, and less experienced man, what my wife would be needing in the coming hours and days.

"Lieutenant," he said, "your lady needs you right now—much more than this brigade does. In her heart, she's probably wondering if she has somehow failed. Let you down. Let herself down. Let her child down."

"Go to her," he said. "Take several days off. Stay with her. Talk to her. Reassure her. Love her."

He asked if I understood. "Yes, sir," I said. "Thank you, sir."

I saluted and turned to go. He stopped me. With a smile and a wink, he said, "Lieutenant...tell her it isn't the end of the world. Tell her Mrs. Smith and I [who had an unusually large and healthy family—the envy of many] have suffered several miscarriages. You can do this. Your future is still very bright. Don't forget that."

With that, I left, having been instructed, encouraged, and deeply touched by a tender warrior. I would be a better man for it. That man on a mission had allowed his tender side to provide perspective. Colonel Smith firmly believed that the whole reason we were soldiers was for our wives, our children, our nation, and our way of life. Again and again through those months under his command, he showed me that without tenderhearted relationships, there was no reason for being a soldier—no reason for anything at all.

There wasn't an ounce of Hollywood in that real-life warrior. No imbalanced machismo. No self-elevating bluster. No trash-talking bravado. No off-the-shelf-hard-guy sneer. Move over Clint Eastwood; I'll let the colonel make my day. Any day.

"A FOND AFFECTION"

Two thousand years ago, another steely-eyed, battle-scarred warrior wrote these words to a group of struggling, persecuted believers in the city of Thessalonica.

> We proved to be gentle among you, as a nursing mother tenderly cares for her own children. Having thus a fond affection for you, we were well-pleased to impart to you not only the gospel

> of God but also our own lives, because you had become very dear to us. (1 Thessalonians 2:7–8)

Gentle? Tender care? Nursing mother? Children? Fond affection? Very dear? Does that sound like a warrior to you? Are those words you would expect from a man's man? God does. Paul says that all his hardship was iron-clad proof of his tender love.

Paul uses a very rare expression to capture his feelings. In all the New Testament, this is the only place this term appears. *Fond affection* is a term taken from the world of the nursery and child care. It is used for the strong endearment of that most gentle of all relationships—a woman and her nursing child. Further, there seems to be a sense of dedicated professionalism attached to its usage. It describes the finest of skilled caregivers. It is that underlying sense of emotional connection required to complete any meaningful challenge—like raising children, for example.

The great apostle suggests that the heart of his ministry was the ministry of his heart—tender, gentle, fond, affectionate. Familial in nature, it elevates a kindred spirit. The one-for-all, all-for-one spirit of the true musketeer. It is a manly skill useful in conquering both continents and gridirons.

Let's go back to that Sunday afternoon football stadium.

Sure, it's only a game, but you'd better believe those massive men in pads and helmets take it seriously. And the best of them know that becoming a champion requires more than passing, catching, running, blocking, and tackling skills. A whole lot more. The blue-chip Sunday warriors recognize that it takes connection, yes, even emotional connection—"fond affection"—to get the job done.

Coaching legend Vince Lombardi (no New Testament theologian by any stretch, but a man who knew men) certainly understood this truth. His Green Bay Packers ran over the top of everybody in professional football in the sixties. And they did it *together,* connected by "fond affection." Lombardi, their leader, insisted upon it. He said it straightforward:

> You've got to care for one another. You have to love one another. Each player has to be thinking about the next guy. The difference between mediocrity and greatness is the feeling these players have for one another. Most people call it team spirit. When the players are imbued with that special feeling you know you have yourself a winning team.[2]

A fond affection overcomes obstacles. It carries. It wins. It literally means "to feel oneself drawn to." It's the kind of emotion our Lord was experiencing when He said to His men, "I have *longed* to have this Passover dinner with you" (see Luke 22:15). *Fond affection* is a term of endearment—an almost uncontrollable urge to hold, to hug, to explode with the joy of togetherness.

It is the hallmark of a tender warrior.

Take It to Heart:

Whether on a football field, in a battle zone, or under the roof of your own home, a man's willingness to show affection and care—to *connect*—mark him as a leader...and a man of God.

Five

UNDER ORDERS

IT WAS ONE OF THOSE golden seasons of life when the sun shines unfailingly warm and the wind blows unfailingly gentle. Linda and I were stationed in what was then West Germany, where I was a brigade officer in an armored division. We had been married less than three years, and our hearts were wrapped around each other and around our bright-eyed, red-cheeked, seven-month-old son. We didn't have much in the way of possessions, but I already had everything I'd ever wanted in life—a loving wife, a baby son, a challenging job, and an outstanding commander.

The envelope should have been no surprise.

We knew it was coming. We knew it *had* to come. Why should my heart pound and my blood run cold when I suddenly received what I knew to be inevitable? And yet…how could I ever be ready to get the ultimate orders to go to Vietnam? Orders that might well be sending me to dismemberment, captivity, or death.

Yet wasn't this what I was trained for? Wasn't this what I was made for? Our nation was at war. What does a soldier do except go into combat?

Six weeks later we were back in Yakima, in my parents' station wagon, riding those few silent miles to the airport. My thirty-day leave was over. Christmas was over. The golden days were over. Forever? Who could say? As the plane climbed up and away, I looked back over my right shoulder. Just for a moment, the little window framed all that was in my heart. My very life. Standing on the tarmac were my mom, my dad, my wife, and my baby. Tiny figures…soon lost from view. I remember thinking, *Why am I doing this? I would rather be doing anything else right now. Of all the places in the world I would rather be, it's the one I'm leaving.*

Finally I had to come back to this: I was doing what I was doing for one reason—I had orders. Like the centurion in Jesus' days, I was a man under authority.

I still am.

No, I'm no longer getting envelopes from the Pentagon, but I am no less a man under authority, a man under orders. And if the Lord God has allowed you the unspeakable privilege of being a husband and father, so are you.

I am a man *in* authority, and I am a man *under* authority. He who is the ultimate authority chose to describe a married man's role in the home as "head." Those were His choice of words, not mine. It is God's word. The orders have been delivered, once for all, to husbands and fathers. We are *commanded* to lead; it isn't optional. Speaking through the apostle, God the Holy Spirit said: "I want you to understand that Christ is the head of every man, and the man is the head of a woman, and God is the head of Christ" (1 Corinthians 11:3).

Here is another passage. The same God is speaking: "For the husband is the head of the wife, as Christ also is the head of the church, He Himself being the Savior of the body" (Ephesians 5:23).

What an astounding, comprehensive statement. As men and husbands, we must own a spirit of submission, not just a sense of technical hierarchy. God has placed us *in* authority, as well as *under* authority. So let me ask you a question or two.

Does it bother a man's wife that "God is the head of Christ"? Probably not. *Does it bother her that "Christ is the head of every man"?* No, in fact she probably loves it and prays it will be more realized every day. *Does it bother a man's wife that "the man is the head of a woman"?* Most likely! Of course it bothers her. Why is that true?

It's probably half due to her sin nature—and half due to *her husband's* sin nature. Why, in our culture, do so many discussions of male/female roles seem so painful, unfair, unreal, unfunny, and even preposterous? Because of men who demand submission from their wives but in turn submit themselves to no one, including God. We men have truncated the process by our arrogant, foolish, egocentric selfishness. We cannot blame women for being frustrated because they fear the injustice of being under headship that itself is not accountable.

Some men draw a big line in the sand and say, "I ain't accountable to nobody, but I am the boss of you." That is neither right nor biblical. Yes, God has given men a certain amount of authority. But we are first and foremost men *under* authority. We always want to quote the verse that says, "The man is the head of a woman." But we conveniently forget the first part of the verse that says, "Christ is the head of every man!" No exceptions. That's me...and you.

Men, are you coming under Christ's authority? That's

the key question of this whole chapter. If as a married man you are not accountable to Christ for your husbanding, you are as guilty as you may feel your wife to be. As a man, as a leader, as a husband, I need to go back to Scripture's admonitions to me that are sandwiched between the instructions to other people to submit. Am I loving my wife as myself? Am I being harsh or inconsiderate with her? Am I exasperating my children with my leadership? Am I embittering them with my unfairness? Am I submitting to the authority of my local church leaders and government authorities? Am I willing to submit myself to fellow Christians? I may think I'm cut out to be a good general, but have I first learned to be a good soldier? Before one can ever lead, he must learn to follow.

If I fail to live as I'm instructed, I undermine my own credibility to remind or teach my family to live as they are instructed.

WHAT'S THE SOLUTION?

When we speak of the biblical headship of the husband, we're dealing with something very fundamental. Masculine headship is universally present. It is the anthropological standard. It is historical practice. Most importantly, it is the scriptural mandate. How then should we respond to it? Accept it and live it. Trust it and obey it. Take the orders and follow them, as men who are under authority.

Yes, many in our culture and in our media kick against it. It is campaigned against, mocked, ridiculed, and even legislated out of fashion. But it will persist. Manhood is here to stay. How tragic though that some Christians, who reputedly accept the authority of Scripture, would resist it.

So what's the solution to all the confusion?

The solution is manly love. Men must develop a thorough, biblical, manly love. Now what is that? In a word, *headship*. It is leadership with an emphasis upon responsibility, duty, and sacrifice—not rank or domination. No "I'm the boss" assertion. Most people who have to insist that they are leader, usually aren't. "Husbands, love your wives *[exactly]* as Christ also loved the church *and gave Himself up for her"* (Ephesians 5:25, emphasis added). Harsh dominance is not the way of Christ.

Note the linkage. Headship is linked to saviorship. The heart of saviorship is sacrifice. The key to leadership is serving, not "lording it over."

Husbands, never shirk your duties as head of your home, but color your headship in soft shades of the tender side...providing, protecting, teaching, caring, guiding, loving, developing, freeing, sacrificing, leading. Do this instead of adopting the harsh tones of the warrior side...ruling, presiding, directing, determining, bossing, deciding.

The essence of the tender tones is servanthood. The mature husband understands servant leadership. Just like Jesus.

Take It to Heart:

God has placed husbands and fathers *in* authority in their own homes, but He has also placed them *under* the authority of Jesus Christ. Until we bow to His lordship and model His sacrificial servanthood, we do not earn the respect necessary to lead.

Six

THE ALONENESS FIGHTER

THE LIVING ONE had been having a ball creating. Earth. Sun. Moon. Stars. Creatures—myriads of them, in a million shapes, sizes, and colors. In His own words, it had been nothing but "good." But then, Scripture tells us, something bothered Him. There was one "not good."

"It is not good for the man to be alone" (Genesis 2:18).

Now Adam hadn't figured that out yet. From his rather limited experience, Adam thought life was rolling along just grandly. Hey, this was paradise. The world smelled new. There was plenty to eat. That was all before God started the parade down Main Street. It was a parade of animals, and that was fun, too, for a while. There they came, waiting to be named, admired, and applauded. There they came, two by two...by two...by two...by two...by two. It wasn't long before this newly minted human being got the picture. He was alone! Flat out by himself. He had no counterpart. All other creatures came in pairs. He did not.

The first little tendrils of loneliness stole across his heart. Life had been full, full, full. What was this place in his chest that felt empty?

Ever been alone? I mean really alone? For a long time? There is nothing worse than aloneness. It is sheer terror. That's why solitary confinement borders on the cruel and unusual. And why it is so effective in breaking down a POW. The Lord said it all with these words: "It is not good for the man to be alone."

But that wasn't the end of His sentence. He went on to add a magnificent promise: "I will make him a helper suitable for him" (Genesis 2:18). And He did. The Creator didn't just snap his fingers and come up with something. In the words of Scripture, He "fashioned" her. He sculpted her. He paid attention to the lines. He worked at it. He created a work of art—mentally, emotionally, physically, and spiritually. She was a "helper suitable."

Ladies, take no offense here. "Helper" is no inferior title. It describes no lesser being. It is not "helper" in the way we might say "plumber's helper." The term says more about the one needing help (the man). It implies the man is incomplete. *He needs help.* As a matter of fact, the God of the universe loves to describe Himself in similar terms—He is our "help" in times of trouble.

"Helper" is a majestic term. And woman is a helper "suitable" or corresponding to the man. That's another way of saying she is no duplicate. Not the same. Not a clone. A woman is not a man with redesigned plumbing. There is no redundancy here. She is *woman.* Glorious. Beautiful. Creative. And different. Adam did not need a buddy, a fishing partner, or another guy to race elephants with. Man needed woman. She is "the rest of the story."

Just how different are we? One gifted woman, Dr. Joyce Brothers, says it clearly: "Are men and women really so different? They are. They really are. I've spent months talking to biologists, neurologists, geneticists, research psychiatrists, and psychologists. What I discovered was that men are more different from women than I had known. Their bodies are different. Their minds are different. Men are different from the very composition of their blood to the way their brains develop, which means they think and experience life differently than women."[3]

More importantly, God says it quite clearly—"male

and female He created them" (Genesis 1:27). Two different words. Two different genders. Two different creatures. No gray, drab world for God. He said, in effect, "Let's dress it up." And women have been doing the same ever since—making things beautiful. Hanging curtains on the bare windows of earth.

Yes, men and women are different. And that very difference combats aloneness.

WALKING TOGETHER

A woman is a companion. She is a friend. *She is an aloneness fighter.* A woman will do almost anything to fight isolation, to combat separation, to overcome aloneness.

I've had the privilege of living with Linda for over thirty years. When I think of all the qualities I appreciate about my wife, I value most her determination not to let us drift apart. But at times it's uncomfortable for me. As a man, there are times when I simply want "my space." And sometimes it has felt as if she is right there in my face. On occasion it has annoyed me that she is always "right there." But she *is* right there. She was made to be there! She is *woman.* She is magnificently woman. Left to myself, I think I would be just that—left to myself, like some bearded, wild-eyed hermit in a back-country lean-to. But the Creator wisely said, "It is not good for the man to be alone."

My wife won't allow me to be isolated. She has become a companion and friend—most often through sheer dogged determination. Fighting aloneness.

Early in our marriage, I really struggled with this. We were married the summer after my junior year and her freshman year in college. The senior year was a busy one for me, finishing up the college experience. There was a lot to conquer and not a lot of time for lingering—at least from my immature perspective. In addition to the normal classroom load, I was captain of the football team and Cadet Brigade Commander in ROTC, traveled in a singing group representing the college, and was finishing up my private pilot's license. I didn't know what "macho" was then, but I had the full-blown disease.

Often while walking across the campus together, Linda would want to hold hands. But my personal and masculine insecurities made it uncomfortable for me. Failing to appreciate her thirst for companionship, I would tend to pull my hand away. Thinking I had to project some kind of football-military-flyboy-tough-guy image, I held her at a distance. Put her off. I mean, *what would "the guys" think?*

Boy, was I ignorant. Completely foolish. Without realizing it, I was wounding the very heart I thought I was willing to die for. Faithful in all the "big things," I was killing her in the little touches. I loved her for a lifetime; I just didn't do so well each day. You know what I mean.

Ah, but life is so daily. And so is my wife. My gracious Lord knows that I need that reminder. I'm so often "out there" climbing trees like Flint McCullough, looking ahead, squinting into the horizon, and planning way down the line. Then Linda reminds me, "I really do look forward to the future with you, but I don't care so much what lifestyle we will have in twenty years. *I want to live with you today.*"

We men can conquer mountains and do large things, but we tend not to do as well at the daily living together and fighting aloneness. Thank God for women! Thank God for the feminine perspective on living relationally. Today I am so very grateful that Linda does not like to walk alone. As recently as last night she said to me, "I like your attention."

Dinah Craik said it so well over a century ago:

Oh, the comfort,
the inexpressible comfort
of feeling safe with another person,
having neither to weigh thoughts
nor measure words,
but pouring them all out,
just as they are,

chaff and grain together,
certain that a faithful hand
will take and sift them,
keep what is worth keeping,
and with a breath of kindness
blow the rest away.

Take It to Heart:

What can a man learn from a woman? That *together* is better and that the path of strength does not lie in isolation and aloneness.

Seven

TAKE HOLD, DAD!

I REMEMBER YEARS AGO standing on the banks of the Yakima River in central Washington. I was just a boy, and boys on riverbanks toss rocks. My dad was with me, and we were throwing rocks together. They would fly farther and farther out into the current with their telltale splashes. It was pretty exciting stuff to see just how far out into this swift, wide river we could wing those missiles.

Then something awesome happened. Dad picked up a rock a little larger than the others. He windmilled it once around his shoulder, stepped into it, and *heaved* that rock like I had not seen before. Wide-eyed, I traced its arc into the sky, watching it seemingly gather power as it flew. And—"holy jumpin' Toledo!"—it cleared the whole river and bounced on the opposite bank. My jaw dropped. To this youngster it was an awe-inspiring display of raw power. My little mind couldn't put it together. But I do remember wondering that day if my dad might really be Clark Kent. Superman. I thought to myself, *I am the son of the most powerful man in the universe.* Everything in me swelled up. I wanted to be just like him. I wanted to walk in my father's shoes.

Little did I know then that my dad's impressive physical strength was just a metaphor of the incredible spiritual strength of a father—a visible symbol of an invisible reality. Like no other person, a father possesses a special power to mold and shape the life of another. All of the basic concepts of character flow from this man's life. Esteem. Principles. Identity. And anchor points. When you think about it awhile, there are few things more powerful.

Consider this astonishing evidence: "When the father is an active believer there is about a seventy-five percent likelihood that the children will also become active believers. But if only the mother is a believer this likelihood is dramatically reduced to fifteen percent."[4]

THE HEART OF MASCULINITY

We've been asking in this little book, "What is a man? What is the heart of masculinity?" If you could picture one word that you could just drop over the top of those basic tenets of manhood, what would it be?

It's *Dad,* isn't it? *Father.*

What a word. What a power-packed word. Is it any wonder all of God's children are taught to pray, "Our Father, who art in heaven..."? God loves to be called "Abba, Father."

What do you remember about your father? I remember my dad's hairy arms. I always wanted hairy arms, like Dad. Silly? No, just a childhood fascination with the nature of masculine maturity in the physical realm, the easiest one for a child to see. I wanted to be like him, and if that meant hairy arms, I couldn't wait.

I remember my dad's body odor. Sound peculiar? Maybe. But you probably do, too. I remember thinking in my little-boy-like way, *I wonder if I'll smell like that someday.* I remember thinking that maybe that was the special scent of our clan, the tribal distinctive, so to speak.

I wanted to pray like my dad prayed. I wanted to understand the Bible the way he understood the Bible. I wanted to grapple with the mystery of "God's plan of the ages," like he always talked about in that grand, admiring tone of voice. I wanted to take hold of life the same way he took hold of life.

Why aren't more men "taking hold" in our country? Why aren't more men showing young hands where to hold on? Could it be that the Industrial Revolution and its aftermath took Dad out of the home entirely? Have we therefore forgotten what dads do? What real men are all about?

Our culture is out of step, out of order. And there's nothing more painful to witness than men who have forgotten what a man is. Dr. Henry Biller speaks a mouthful when he says, "The principle danger to fatherhood today is that fathers do not have the vital sense of father power that they had in the past. Because of a host of pressures from society, the father has lost the confidence that he is naturally important to his children, that he has the power to affect children, to guide them and help them grow. He isn't confident that fatherhood is a basic part of being masculine and the legitimate focus of his life."[5]

At the root of masculinity is fatherhood. But think of that term in large rather than narrow terms. *Even if you don't have children of your own, you can still father.* Fathering is a vast field. The easiest aspect of fatherhood is the most obvious and physical—reproducing children biologically. But fathering has only a little to do with biology. At its heart, it has everything to do with originating, influencing, and shaping. I believe that if we understand it rightly, we will conclude that every man is, at his soul level, a father—whether he has biological children or not.

Father. Look the word right in the eye. Webster is straightforward in his definition: "One who has begotten a child; one who cares for; one to whom respect is due; an originator; a source."

Personally, I believe father has more to do with the "caring" than the "begetting." Begetting can take place in a thoughtless moment of passion. Fathering never will. Begetting can be utterly selfish. Fathering never can.

The verb form of *father* is even more strikingly potent: "To beget. To be a founder. To be the foundation. To author." Think through the implications of that verb—*father*—in your home, workplace, or in the affairs of daily living. To father is to be one who puts together the scope and sequence of life. To be the one who authors the curriculum for the development of generations to come. To be the author. To accept responsibility for.

To take hold! To grip groping young hands with tender strength and hold on until young feet have confidence on the sometimes dark, sometimes slippery path.

How powerfully we are affected by our fathers—present or absent, negative or positive. And it isn't just boys who feel both the waves and undertow of that vast force. Listen to this heart-wrenching letter I received from a dear woman in our congregation.

> My dad was what I thought was a real man.... He was the provider and worked hard for our physical needs. He had to go 150 miles away from home to find work, coming home often only on weekends.... As could be expected, I didn't know my dad very well.
>
> When I reached adolescence, I began to desire more than anything to win his approval. It became an all-consuming need. I went back and forth from being a tomboy to being feminine to try to get him to like me. I took up fishing and made myself pull apart worms and get slime under my fingernails so that I could bait my own hooks and we could go fishing. But he didn't have time to go fishing anymore.
>
> I started playing softball and became the best pitcher in our school. But he never saw me play a game. I worked hard to get straight A's and was always on the honor roll. Never once did he say he was proud of me. One year I was a cheerleader. He never came to a game. One year I was captain of the drill team. He never saw a performance.

> One weekend I tried to help him work on the car. But he was cross with me and I was in the way. I went into the house and made some cookies. He said I baked them too long.
>
> More and more I found myself retreating to my room on the weekends, sobbing violently, wanting him to care. Not once did he comfort me. He never read to me. He never tucked me into bed. He never hugged me. He never kissed me. He never said, "I love you."

Later in life, after she had raised four kids, she went back to work. She writes,

> Somehow, without meaning to, I found myself studying civil engineering, the field of study closest to his profession. I worked as a surveyor last year laying out lines just like the lines he had put in for years. I found myself thinking, *If he could see me, he'd be proud of me.*

What power a father has over the direction of a daughter's life! Good or bad, present or absent, his influence lasts a lifetime. I think a lot of fathers leave their daughters to the mothers to raise, thinking a man's influence isn't necessary for girls.

> I'm thirty-seven years old now and beginning to see how much I am still compelled by a deep craving within to gain the approval of this most significant man. You see, if my own father doesn't think I'm worthwhile, I must be worthless. If my own father can't accept me, then I am unacceptable. If my own father cannot love me, then I must be totally unlovable. If I'm truly worthless and unacceptable and unlovable, then God couldn't really love me. And certainly my dear husband, who is only human, couldn't really love me.
>
> I thank God that He's opening my eyes to these lies and showing me His truth. He has begun the process of healing, but the wounds are really deep. I fear the effects of the scarring will be with me while I remain on this earth.

They probably will. And they will likely touch those four kids, too. And their kids. That's the incredible power of fathering. It extends transgenerationally to the third and fourth generations.

Take hold, Dad! Take hold now, while there's still time to make a difference.

Need some suggestions to get you started? Try these on for size.

1. Pursue the ultimate Father.

That was my father's focus—and my grampa's before him. Live for eternity instead of the weekends. Think mission. Think larger than yourself. Give your life away to the ultimate Father and the people He has sovereignly placed around you. Whether you are married or not, or have children or not, you are a man. You were made to be with other people—a provider, protector, teacher, and friend. Go for it.

2. Model and teach respect for authority.

A father is a source, a founder, an author. *Author* is the root of *authority.* A father is an authority and represents the ultimate Author, the ultimate Authority. Teach your children to respect each other, all others, adults in general, and schoolteachers in particular.

3. Help your family see the big picture.

Show your kids how God sees this world. Help them wrestle with eternal perspective. Teach them that life is so much more than holding a job and living at an address. It is a mission—living for the Kingdom! Get involved in a local church—one that takes the Bible, itself, and you seriously.

4. *Commit solidly to family unity.*

Help everyone understand that there will be no isolation or enmity under your roof. Nip it in the bud. Root it out wherever it raises its head. We have a little saying at our house that we repeat regularly: "We will never do it perfectly around here, but we will always do it together."

5. *Be positive in building family members' confidence.*

"You know, honey...you know, son...you are the only you. There'll never be another like you. You have passions, interests, talents, and gifts that make a unique contribution. I appreciate you and the way you are. I learn from you."

Wow! What an opportunity! Make the most of it. Whatever your job or status in life might be, you have no greater—or more powerful—privilege. Take hold, Dad!

"LET'S RUN TOGETHER"

My own dad's physical strength showed up in a lot of projects, chores, and things such as throwing rocks across rivers. But one day in particular, I was struck again with that strength and how it could touch me.

Down the hill from our house was a vacant lot. On one occasion, Dad and I were down there together. We might have been playing catch; I don't remember exactly.

But I'll never forget the run up the hill.

In the midst of our activity, Mom came to the front porch of old "3309" (an affectionate reference to our home) and called us to dinner. Dad and I glanced at each other. Our eyes met—and sparkled. Without a word, we both sensed it was time for a race. We took off. It was about 150 yards uphill to the house. It was glorious running along with my dad. Man, it was great! But try as I might, my little legs couldn't keep up with his long ones. He started to pull ahead. My neck strained and my muscles stretched, but I was losing ground. Then something really special happened.

Dad, seeing me start to drop back, reached out his hand to me.

His eyes said, *Grab hold. Let's run together.*

Still running, my little hand slipped inside his larger one. It was like magic! His power lifted me right off the ground. I took off in his strength. My speed doubled because my dad had hold of me.

That's a lot like life. A kid's speed doubles when Dad takes hold at home. *Take hold,* Dad! Hold on for all you're worth. Hold on in the face of storms and disappointments and sorrows and temptations and hurts and crazy, churning circumstances. There isn't much of anything in life children can't face with Dad's strong hand wrapped tightly around theirs.

And while you're at it, with your other hand, hold on tightly to your heavenly Father's hand. Let Him be your confidence and wisdom and stability when you just can't find your own. Let His strength pull you up life's long hills until you stand together, laughing and catching your breath, on heaven's front porch.

Isn't that what dads are for?

Take It to Heart:

Fatherhood is the very heart of masculinity. We are never stronger than when we grip the hands of those who look to us for strength.

Eight

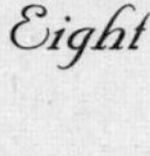

Real Men Stand Together

DOWN DEEP AT THE CORE, every man needs a friend.

Down deep at the core, every man needs a brother to lock arms with.

Down deep at the core, every man needs a soul mate.

Yes, beyond question, a man's wife is designed by God to be his most intimate companion. And once we're married, you and I are to be willing to die for our wives and our children instantly, and many of us are ready to do just that. But within the willingness to die for family and home, something inside us longs for someone to die *with*...someone to die *beside*...someone to lock step with. Another man with a heart like our own.

Every warrior needs a fellow soldier. Every fighter pilot needs a wingman. Even the U.S. Army, in all its relational apathy ("we don't care how you feel"), understands this. When you're going to do something that stretches the fabric of your soul—like get through nine weeks of army Ranger school at Fort Benning, Georgia—you're going to need a buddy. A "Ranger Buddy."

Those two words mean a world to me. It was my Ranger Buddy, Lou Francis, who clung to my arm and I to his through sixty-three days of unbelievable physical and mental trauma. Together, we made it through the toughest experience either of us had ever encountered up to that point in our lives.

Some might argue with me, but I know of no more intense training regimen in the U.S. military. These guys know how to take a young man and stretch him tendon by tendon—physical tendon by physical tendon, emotional tendon by emotional tendon.

I remember well the last, most intense phase of our training. We were in the swamps of western Florida in the dead of winter. I would never have dreamed that Florida could be so cold. We were at the end of a several-day patrol and nearly at the end of ourselves. We'd been without sleep for most of those days and very nearly without food. Our particular mission required us to proceed to a certain set of coordinates at the corner of our map. Unfortunately, those coordinates happened to be on the other side of the Yellow River.

We had been staggering knee-deep through the numbing water of a cypress swamp for what seemed like eons. The temperature was below freezing, and our bodies were at the ragged edge of our endurance. The "knees" of the cypress trees, invisible under the black waters, savaged our shins and ankles.

When we finally reached the river, it was practically indistinguishable from the water we'd been wading in. The only way we could tell it was a river was by the rapidly moving current and the lack of cypress trees.

Our goal was a piece of higher ground on the other side. We knew we couldn't get our clothes wet or the cold would finish us. So we stripped down to our skimpy briefs and, as we'd been trained, made a little float out of our two ponchos, with our rifles and packs protected. Wading out into the icy water, we were surprised by the strength of the current. Though we were both fair swimmers, we found ourselves being swept further and further downstream. It was fearsome. Reaching back for a burst of strength from some final untapped reserve, both of us began kicking with all our might. The effort was rewarded as we inched toward the slimy bank and finally achieved it.

We crawled out of the water, blue from the cold, trailing bits of river weed and slime. So delighted to be alive. So exultant at having reached our goal. I remember our looking into each other's eyes and then spontaneously throwing our arms around each other. We stood there for a moment on the bleak winter bank of the Yellow River, two dripping, shivering young men in their briefs, laughing and crying and holding on to each other as if we'd never let go.

If we each live to be a hundred, I expect neither of us will ever forget the camaraderie of that moment. We'd made it. We'd stayed alive. The two of us.

Every man, whether he admits it or not, needs a Ranger Buddy. Every man needs someone with whom he can face adversity and death. Emerson wrote: "We take care of health. We lay up money. We make our roof tight. We make our clothing sufficient. But who provides wisely that he shall not be wanting in the best property of all, friends—friends strong and true?"

WHY MEN DON'T CULTIVATE FRIENDS

A professor at Southern Methodist University had this to say after ten years of study on the subject: "To say that men have no intimate friends seems on the surface too harsh, and it raises quick objections from most men. But the data indicates that it is not far from the truth. Even the most intimate of friendships (of which there are few) rarely approach the depth of disclosure a woman commonly has with other women...men, who neither bare themselves nor bear one another, are buddies in name only."[6]

Oh, we may *want* that friendship. Every man, whether he admits it or not, walks around with a hollow place in his chest, wondering if he is the only one. But there is something within us that keeps us at arm's length. *What is that something that keeps men distant and friendless?*

Patrick Morley wryly observes that although most men could recruit six pallbearers, "hardly anyone has a friend he can call at 2:00 A.M."[7] Sociologist Marion Crawford stated that middle-aged men and women have considerably different definitions of friendship. By an overwhelming margin, women talked about "trust and confidentiality," while men described a friend as "someone I could go out with" or "someone whose company I enjoy." For the most part, men's friendships revolve around activities—golfing buddies, fishing buddies—while women's revolve around sharing.

Why are these things true? I have my theories. If we men are comprised of steel and velvet, most of us feel more comfortable with the steel...the hard side dominates the tender side. Many of us have underdeveloped tender sides because we've been taught wrongly about manhood. Not deliberately, but wrongly. We need to become more tender. The warrior in us wants to be strong and needs to be strong. But we don't want to admit to any chinks in our armor. We don't want to admit to any vulnerabilities—*the very element that is essential for true friendships.* Oh, the vulnerabilities are there, all right. But most of us have learned to carefully hide them. Some might call that "manliness." Others might more accurately label it for what it is: *dishonesty.*

Friendship requires honesty. Friendship requires trust. So it also—no way around it—requires vulnerability. I think that's the bottom line of this no-friends syndrome in us men. And it's spelled P-R-I-D-E.

We all want to think of ourselves as some kind of warrior, as some kind of John Wayne man's man. Unfortunately though, as much as we love John Wayne, there is a side to the Duke that never emerged. All you ever saw was the steel. You never saw the velvet, unless it was for a fleeting moment in *She Wore a Yellow Ribbon.*

John Wayne left us with the impression that real men stand alone. And they do...when it is necessary. But the only reason it seems "necessary" most of the time is our stubborn, unyielding pride.

Real men stand together. We need to start thinking that way. Real men need one another. Real soldiers love each other.

Let's face it, though: Most of us are rusty when it comes to sharing our emotions. We need practice. We need to work at it a little. May I offer a suggestion here? Find somebody who seems more relaxed and skilled at it, and watch how they do it. Find some moment in your week that's been especially emotional for you, and then pick out that friend whose name is turning over in your mind and heart today, and go share your emotions with that friend. Start at whatever level. If you need to prime the pump, start with your wife. Most women would really treasure a husband's attempt to climb out of his shell.

When you open your Bible, spend some time in the Psalms with David. Here was a true man's man and mighty warrior who knew how to put his emotions into words. David also knew how to spill his guts before God. He knew how to cry out his fears and discouragements and hopes and joys. You can see the whole range of feelings in this man's words. Joyful laughter. Shouts of praise. Burning anger. The deep hurt of betrayal. Paralyzing fear.

Overwhelming waves of discouragement. Sweet relief. Overflowing gratitude. Love. It's all there. He's all over the emotional, spiritual map. His journey is the spiritual journey of a tender warrior, recorded forever in Scripture for warriors like you and me who want to follow in his wake.

When my father was in World War II, he made friends with a young man named Joe Carter. They were young draftees, plucked out of a peaceful civilian life and thrown into the same barracks at training camp. For a good chunk of the war, they were together. Serving together. Sweating together. Dreaming together of home. It has been over fifty years since they last saw each other. But every year, without fail, my dad gets a birthday card from Joe Carter in the mail.

It's hard to believe that friendship started when my dad walked across the barracks one afternoon to offer a guy named Joe one of the chocolate-chip cookies he'd just received in a package from home. Dad's now in his seventies. And every once in a while, he will pause and look out the window with a distant stare. Then with a smile on the corners of his lips, he'll say, "You know...I should grab a train and go see my friend Joe."

A fifty-year friendship sprang from a single chocolate chip cookie. It's that way sometimes. All it takes is breaking the ice. All it takes is walking across the barracks. Or across the hall. Or across the street. Or across the room to pick up the phone. It takes a willingness to choke back some pride and reach out a hand.

Are you giving yourself to anyone? Are you opening up to anyone? Do any of your fellow soldiers know where the chinks in your armor might be? Are you looking for a soul mate, a Ranger Buddy?

Some dark day when your knees are weak, the current is swift, and the water is cold, you will be glad you did.

Take It to Heart:

Every warrior has chinks in his armor. Admitting vulnerabilities to a trusted friend provides protection and hope, a shield on days when darkness falls and arrows fly.

Nine

The Ultimate Tender Warrior

ONE OF THE CHOICEST SNAPSHOTS in my mental album dates from a moment when I was half a world away from the event.

It happened about four decades ago while I was slogging through the deltas and jungles of Southeast Asia. My father was playing the role with my one-year-old son that I would have loved to have been playing. Little Kent and his grandpa were wrestling and rolling around on the carpet like grandpas and grandsons are supposed to do.

In the course of all that thrashing about, one of Kent's fingers inadvertently scratched my father's eye.

It didn't hurt much, but Dad decided to take advantage of the situation and to appeal to this little one. Down on his knees, Dad dropped his head to the floor and buried his face in the carpet. He covered the sides of his face with his hands and began howling and carrying on, as if in great distress.

Little Kent, however, had already picked up a few things about life. In a life span of twelve months, he'd begun to learn something about grandpas—and men. So he got down on the carpet as close as he could to his grandpa's face. He kept trying to pull those big hands away from the hidden face so he could look into his grandpa's eyes.

"Aw, Bompa," my boy said. "Be a *big* bompa."

Kent knew something about bompas. About big men. About strong men. He had some expectations. His grandpa was a grown man, and Kent was expecting something of him. My little guy was already becoming alert to the masculine qualities of strength and courage. And in his one-year-old owning of this thing called masculinity, he was trying to impart courage to another human being.

Come on, Bompa. Be a big bompa. Big bompas can take the rough and tumble. Big bompas can absorb the hits and bounce back. Big bompas are supposed to be strong, stable, and provide direction...not whine around on the carpet.

Joe Stowell, president of Moody Bible Institute, writes, "I was born male. But early in my life, I learned that being male did not necessarily make me a *man.* I realized this the first time somebody said, 'Joe, be a man.' It was probably when I had started crying or refused to eat my spinach. I discovered that I had a new task in life: to go beyond just being a male and discover what it means to be a 'man.'"[8]

As we approach the last few steps of this little journey together, let's fill our vision with another young Man, learning to be what He was meant to be.

THE CALLING

Remember when, at the age of twelve, Jesus became separated from His parents at a festival in Jerusalem? After searching for Him for three days, "they found Him in the temple, sitting in the midst of the teachers, both listening to them, and asking them questions" (Luke 2:46). Joseph and Mary were astonished at this turn of events, and His mother said to Him, "Son, why have You treated us this way? Behold, Your father and I have been anxiously looking for You" (v. 48).

And do you remember His answer? "Why did you seek Me? Did you not know that I must be about My Father's business?" (v. 49, NKJV).

Jesus was a boy beginning to assert His calling. He was fast becoming a man. He was fast living out what He had come to earth for. He was saying to Mary and Joseph, in essence, "Why are you surprised? Why would you be looking for Me anywhere else? Don't you know I was born for this? This is who I am; this is what I do. Is it so surprising to you?"

There was a sense of destiny about this twelve-year-old. It is an inner equilibrium increasingly hard to find among the boys and men of our culture. These are days when men are "looking for themselves." Adrift. I sometimes picture a vessel with no prow, no stern, no rudder, and—worse yet—no *keel.* I picture men with a single oar in the water, paddling here and there. Solemnly going around and around in circles. Going nowhere at all and despising every moment of the fruitless journey.

Where do you go to find the keel of manhood? Where do you go to find the rudder with which to steer your masculinity? Where do you find the zenith, the epitome of manliness?

All kinds of false models are out there. Where is the real? I suggest what should already be obvious. Jesus Christ is the ultimate Man. Maximum manhood. The perfect Model. The complete Hero.

Why is it that when someone says, "Picture the archetypal male," the image that comes to mind is *not* one of Jesus? Why is that? I have to confess that, for years, the picture in my mind would not have been Jesus. It wouldn't have occurred to me. Why? I think it's because we've looked in all the wrong places for our images of manhood. We've allowed our vision of Jesus to be truncated by Hollywood and a media that either hates and distorts Him or vastly misunderstands Him. We've developed our images of the God-man in the darkness of the uncaring and uninformed.

Even the single most famous "portrait" of Jesus makes Him look more like a pouting model for Breck shampoo than a man. Doesn't it? His eyes aren't toward you. The face is thin and aloof. The long hair is waved and feminine.

That's not the Jesus of the Bible! Somehow we've allowed Him to be painted as "gentle Jesus meek and mild" or "the pale Galilean." He is so much more than those images. He is very real. Forever relevant. And if I read the Bible correctly, fully human.

My visual picture of Christ's masculinity changed forever when I visited Israel for the first time almost thirty years ago. The Breck shampoo ads fell off my mental screen when we stepped off the plane and met David (pronounced DaVEED), the driver for our group. I watched David for nine weeks. He was a twenty-five-year-old Jewish male in his prime, a native-born *sabra.* That's the modern Hebrew term for a prickly pear cactus: tough on the outside, tender and sweet within. David's skin was dark. Dark by pigment, dark by the bronzing of the sun. His hair was black, medium length, somewhat wavy. It hung naturally on his head and matted on his forehead in the afternoon heat.

More than anything else, I noticed his eyes. Very dark. Sometimes hard as black steel, sometimes soft, with smiles dancing on the edges. Piercing eyes. Kind eyes. Intelligent eyes. Eyes brimming with life. David was so serious and so hilarious all at the same time that we were irresistibly drawn to him. He had just been released from the hospital, where he had been convalescing from wounds suffered in the Yom Kippur War. I'll never forget the picture he made as he first stood before us...clad in neat khakis, arms folded, legs apart, smiling a welcome. In love with life, in love with his family, in love with his people and nation.

As we became acquainted, my mind was drawn back to another "Daveed," three thousand years previous, from the same gene pool. That David had been a great warrior, the complete Hebrew man of his day. In love with life, his family, his nation, and his God. From that

David, it wasn't much of a mental jump to cross a thousand years to the greater Son of David, Jesus of Nazareth, the ultimate King, Warrior, Mentor, and Friend.

Three men, all with the same origin, all from the same covenant people. Without consciously trying to adjust the mental image, I found myself thinking differently of Jesus. The pale, limp-wristed Galilean faded like a bad dream and the laughing, dark-skinned Son of God took over the picture in my mind. The greater *Sabra.* The real Tender Warrior.

THE HEART OF JESUS' MANHOOD: PURPOSE

There was a sense of purpose in Jesus. A clarity of vision. A force of direction.

Men today are searching. That's obvious. But all the searching in the world is no good if you're not looking in the right place. Conspicuous by its absence in so many men today is that strong, motivating sense of purpose. No vision shimmers on the horizon. No mountain peaks call from the purple distance. No steely convictions glint in the eyes. There is only confusion and mist...a soft fog of self-talk with neither direction nor resolution.

The single thing that marks every aspect of Jesus' life was a driving sense of cause. "*This* is who I am, *this* is what I do, *this* is where I am going...*and why don't you come, too?*"

He was a man on a mission. That's what swept strong men along in His wake. That's what persuaded them in a heartbeat to drop their fishing nets or hammers or ledgers or whatever else they were doing and follow Him. Suddenly whatever had preoccupied them seemed pallid and tame and slightly irrelevant. The Man who called them was burning Reality. A Great Light. How could they help but follow along?

A real man knows where he is going.

Dr. Luke offers this revealing snapshot in chapter 9 of his gospel: "And it came about, when the days were approaching for His ascension, that He resolutely set His face to go to Jerusalem.... He was journeying with His face toward Jerusalem" (vv. 51, 53).

He set His face. He locked His eyes. He cemented His direction. He was going somewhere. He owned an unshakable purpose. He set His face to go to Jerusalem, knowing full well what faced Him there—hatred and ridicule and torture and the unspeakable sin and rebellion of all the world for all time seared into His being. Blacker by far than any of these shadows, He faced the rejection and searing wrath of His own Father. But even those prospects did not slow His feet or weaken His resolve. He was willing to pay the ultimate price because He was a man on a mission.

In John 19:30, we see the final, blinding burst of that

flaming resolve. This time, the God-man was hanging on a cross. To those around Him, He looked like a victim. He was anything but a victim. Submerged as He was in a sea of pain and horror, He was so alert to the tiny particulars of Scripture that He whispered "I thirst," to the soldiers who gazed at Him from below (see verse 28). The vinegar found its way to His parched lips, and when that was done, having accomplished it all, He cried with a loud voice, "It is finished!"

It wasn't a whimper. It wasn't a sigh of resignation. It was a shout of triumph that shook the cosmos from the dungeons of hell to the corona of Alpha Centauri.

"It's Done!"

And so it was. The mission was completed. He had accomplished what He had come to do. He had wrapped up His Father's business. A few hours earlier, anticipating that moment, He had lifted His eyes to heaven and said, "I have accomplished the work You have given Me to do" (see John 17:4).

That's the heart of what makes a man. That ringing sense of destiny. That soul-seizing challenge to overcome. To conquer for a cause.

A man, you see, was made for a cause. A man was made for something outside of himself. A man was made for something beyond. That's why so many of us draw a disproportionate sense of achievement from our jobs, ordinary as they may be. And that's why so many newly retired men suddenly find life tasteless and empty. Through all their years, they have completely attached their masculine identity to the Wedgwood Lumber Company or the Pushpenny National Bank or the Western Widget Consortium. Then, when they have worked their thirty or forty years and collected their gold watch, it's done. Their job is over, and so is their reason for living! What is left to do but tuck your watch in the top drawer, lie in your bed, draw up your legs, and die?

What a prostitution of the image of God in man! What a needless tragedy! For the cause of Christ *never* dies. Never lessens its call on a man's life. Never ceases to throb with urgency as time rushes on its short track toward eternity.

The cause is eternal. The kingdom is out there. Kingdom deeds await doing in the borrowed might of the Almighty. If you and I keep trying to attach our purpose for living to some workaday profession or nine-to-five job, we forfeit the heart of true masculinity. *No wonder* so many of us become frustrated in our careers and find ourselves on the canyon rim of life crises. *No wonder* we find ourselves numbed at times by the crushing emptiness of it all. We're looking for purpose; we were made for a purpose, and our puny jobs just aren't *big* enough to slake that thirst.

What do you see, after all, when you look at the vehicle of a man's physical body? What was it made for? Check it out. In contrast, what does a woman's body tell you a woman was made for? Every twenty-eight days or so, her body tells her she was made for giving life. Her breasts remind her that she was made for nurturing life. What does a man's body tell you?

Not a thing! Why? Because the purpose for a man is out on the horizon. A man was made to be a provisionary, a wagon scout, out there in front, looking ahead. The purpose isn't inside.

We must find that purpose outside ourselves. We must find it in Him.

Men, you and I need to own for ourselves that same clarity of vision that so marked the life of Christ. We need to give ourselves up for our brides and *the* Bride as He did. So that the family might be healthy. So that the people might live well. So that this nation might continue to experience His favor and remain the land of the free.

There are some little guys and gals out there who need big bompas. There are some women out there who need clear-eyed provisionaries—men who face the worst hell has to throw at them and stay and stay and stay.

There's a world out there that needs some tender warriors. It's every man's purpose...every woman's dream...and every child's hope. It's the definition of a man. I want to head down that road with all my heart. But I want some Ranger Buddies to walk with me. Will you come? Let's do it together.

Take It to Heart:

A man was made for a purpose beyond himself. When we give ourselves irrevocably to the ultimate Tender Warrior, we find the vision, purpose, and direction to sustain us for a lifetime. Seek Christ and follow Him.

Take It to Heart

1

Along the way, every one of us will find ourselves in situations that shake us to the core—and cause us to think about the critical issues of life. But why wait until circumstances crush us? *Now* is the time to wake up and seek God's help, wisdom, and direction.

2

God expects men to be providers in the most complete sense of the word...leaders with eyes on the horizon, anticipating the perils, smelling hope in the wind, and inspiring loved ones to follow.

3

The true measure of a man is not in his physical power, in the skill of his hands, in the quickness of his wit, or in his ability to pile up possessions. True, manly courage is best seen in his willingness to make and keep promises—though all hell should oppose him.

4

Whether on a football field, in a battle zone, or under the roof of your own home, a man's willingness to show affection and care—to *connect*—mark him as a leader...and a man of God.

5

God has placed husbands and fathers *in* authority in their own homes, but He has also placed them *under* the authority of Jesus Christ. Until we bow to His lordship and model His sacrificial servanthood, we do not earn the respect necessary to lead.

6

What can a man learn from a woman? That *together* is better and that the path of strength does not lie in isolation and aloneness.

7

Fatherhood is the very heart of masculinity. We are never stronger than when we grip the hands of those who look to us for strength.

8

Every warrior has chinks in his armor. Admitting vulnerabilities to a trusted friend provides protection and hope, a shield on days when darkness falls and arrows fly.

9

A man was made for a purpose beyond himself. When we give ourselves irrevocably to the ultimate Tender Warrior, we find the vision, purpose, and direction to sustain us for a lifetime. Seek Christ and follow Him.

to Contact Stu Weber,
write him at
2229 E. Burnside, #212
Gresham, Oregon 97080

NOTES

1. Lewis Smedes, "The Power of Promising," *Christianity Today,* 21 January 1983, 16–17.

2. From Stu: "I've seen this statement from Vince Lombardi on desk tops, office walls, and slips of paper in wallets, but I've never been able to locate its original source."

3. Dr. Joyce Brothers, *What Every Woman Should Know about Men* (New York: Simon and Schuster, 1981), 11–13.

4. Keith Meyering in an interview in "The Small Group Letter," *Discipleship Journal* 49 (1989): 41.

5. As quoted in Dave Simmons, *Dad the Family Coach* (Wheaton, Ill.: Victor Books, 1990), 31.

6. Michael E. McGill, *The McGill Report on Male Intimacy* (New York: Holt, Rinehart and Winston, 1985), 157–158.

7. Patrick Morley, *The Man in the Mirror* (Brentwood: Wolgemuth & Hyatt, 1989), 117.

8. Joseph M. Stowell, "The Making of a Man," *Moody Monthly,* May 1992, 4.